A Treasury of
Hanukah
Games

Tamar TalShir

A Treasury of Hanukah Games

Design: Haim Ron

Adama Books

Copyright © 1989 Adama Books
All rights reserved

A Treasury of Hanukah Games /
by Tamar TalShir

ISBN 1-55774-033-X

Design by Haim Ron
Plates by Yacov & Shlomo Nakar - Y.SH. OFFSET
Printed in Israel
Adama Books, 306 West 38 Street, New York, New York 10018

A Treasury of Hanukah Games

Hanukah is a family holiday, celebrated during the cold winter months. Adama Publishing is happy to present you with a variety of entertaining games for this enjoyable holiday, incorporating the traditional Hanukah symbols of dreidls, foods, Hanukah "gelt," the Maccabbees and the Temple.

The games are suitable for school-age children and up, and most are designed for two to four players. Some of the games are based on knowledge, while others combine strategy and luck. Most of the games are of brief duration and provide a pleasant family experience.

Preparation

Where indicated, cut along the dotted lines, to create the elements of the game. Equip yourself with coins, dreidl and dice.

INDEX

4 DREIDL GAMES

The following games are based on the motifs of ancient dreidl games.

Game 1

Object of the game: To win all the disks, or any number established in advance by the players.
Number of players: 2 to 4
Equipment: 36 disks (or candies, matchsticks, coins or the like)
                    A box for the disks
                    One dreidl (or a dreidl for each player)

Directions for Play

Distribute the disks evenly among all the players. Place the box in the center of the table.
At each player's turn, all the players place 1 to 3 disks in the box. The player whose turn it is has to bet on which letter the dreidl will fall, then he spins the dreidl. If the letter he predicted is the one which turns up, he takes all the disks in the box. If not, play passes to the next player, and all put 1 to 3 disks in the box again. If this player bets on the correct letter, he takes all the disks in the box.

Winner

Play continues in this way until one player either wins all the disks or the number which had been decided upon in advance.

Variations

- Place only one disk in the box on each turn.
- See that each player has his own dreidl. All spin at the same time, each betting on a letter. The one whose dreidl lands on the letter which he bet takes all the disks in the box. If more than one person succeeds in his bet, the disks are divided evenly among those who succeeded. The uneven portion of disks remains in the box.

Game 2

Object, equipment and number of players are the same as in Game 1.

Directions for Play

The disks are divided evenly among all the players. The box is placed in the center of the table.

At each turn, all players place one disk in the box. Each player, in turn, spins the dreidl and wins or loses according to the following system:

נ = nothing. No disks won or added.
ג = everything. The player takes all disks in the box.
ה = half. The player takes half the disks in the box.
ש = put. The player must put half of his own disks in the box.

If there is an uneven number of disks, subtract one, then divide in half. For example, if a player has 7 disks and he must place half of them in the box, set one aside so there are 6, then divide in half. This means he must put 3 disks in the box.

Winner

The player who wins all the disks in the box or reaches the number of disks which had ben determined in advance.

Game 3

Object of the game: To be the first to reach 1000 points.
Number of players: 2 to 4
Equipment: dreidl
                     paper and pencil

Directions for Play

List the names of each player on a sheet of paper, across the top of the page (so scores can be written in columns). Each player, in turn, spins the dreidl and receives a score according to the letter's value in "gimetria."

נ = 50
ג = 3
ה = 5
ש = 300

Winner

The first player to reach 1000 points.

Game 4

Object of the game: To score 10 points
Number of Players: 2 to 4
Equipment: dreidl, pencil and paper

Directions for Play

Each player, in turn, before spinning the dreidl, has to bet whether the letter on which the dreidl will fall will be "above 30" or "below 30". For example, if he bets "above 30" and the dreidl falls on ה, whose value is 5, or ג, whose value is 3, he scores no point. If, instead, it falls on נ, whose value is 50, or ש, whose value is 300, he scores a point.

Winner

The first player to reach 10 points.

Belongs —
Doesn't Belong

Educational purpose: Identifying characteristics of the various holidays
(the New Year period, Hanukah, Passover), memory development
Object of the game: to collect 4 cards giving characteristics of the selected holiday
(explained under Directions for Play)
Number of players: 2
Equipment   Hexagon board
            24 cards (8 cards for each holiday)
            1 playing piece
            1 die

Directions for Play

1. Lay out the cards face down on the hexagons of the board, except for the center one.
2. Set the playing piece on one of the circles surrounding the central hexagon.
3. The players decide which series of cards to collect (each series has 8 cards). If playing the game during Hanukah, for example, then the object of the game is to collect the Hanukah series.
4. Each player, in turn, rolls the die and moves the playing piece according to the number on the die, from one circle to the next
5. When landing on a circle, the player can lift one of the three cards whose edges are in the circle. (If the playing piece is at the edge of the board, only two cards are available.) If the player lifts a card which he needs, that is, one connected to the right holiday, he keeps the card. Play passes to the second player. If the card is not one which he needs, he shows it to the second player, then returns it to its place, face down. Play passes to the second player.

Winner

The first player to collect 4 cards related to the chosen holiday.

2 Dreidls and a Menorah

Educational purpose: Learning to identify and read the letters (נ.ג.ה.ש)
Object of the game: Each player tries to "light" the greatest number of candles with his color and score the greatest number of points.
Number of players: 2
Equipment: 9 flames; each flame is made up of two colors
                2 dreidls

Directions for Play

Each player chooses a color. Each player, in turn, spins 2 dreidls. If both fall on the same letter, the player places his color on the "shammes". If the other player's color is already there, he turns the color over to his own. If the letters are not identical, the color is placed (or turned over) on the candle showing that combination of letters.

FOR EXAMPLE: If the dreidls fall on a combination of letters for which a "flame" has not yet been placed on the candle, the player places his color on the candle. If the other player's color already is on the candle, he turns it over so that his color is facing up.

NOTE: The letter combinations of נ+ג and ה+ש appear twice.

Conclusion

The game is completed when all the "flames" have been "lit." Total the points of each player. Each regular candle counts as 1 point. The "shammes" counts as two points. The player with the highest total of points is the winner.

Hanukah
Candles

Educational purpose: To learn thoroughly the story of Hanukah.
Object of the game: To be the first to cover the board of 8 candles.
Number of players: 2
Equipment   Menorah board (upon which are the answers)
                 16 cards — "candles" of various sizes upon which are the
                 questions
                 control board

Directions for Play

Each player, in turn, takes a card and reads the question on it out loud. If the
answer is on his board, he reads out the answer, then places the candle on it,
with the question facing down (the size of the candle on the card matches the
outline on the board). If the answer is on the second player's board, the second
player reads out the answer then receives the candle card for his board. Note
that the size of the candle on the question card and the outline of the answer
section of the board match each other exactly.

Winner

The first player to cover his board with 8 candles.

Spin & Spell

Educational purpose: Improving spelling by matching letters with words
Number of players: 2 to 4
Equipment: dreidl-track board
                4 word cards
                4 playing pieces
                1 dreidl
                paper and pencil for each player

Directions for Play

Each player chooses a playing piece and places it on the starting arrow.
Each player takes a word card to complete.
Each player, in turn, spins the dreidl then moves the playing piece according to the value of the letter on which it falls:

נ = 4
ג = 3
ה = 2
ש = 1

Each player can move in the direction of his choice. When a player lands on a letter which belongs to one of the words on his card, he writes it down on his card. If the player lands on a letter which he does not need, he can skip to another part of the board where the same letter appears. This ends his turn, and play passes to the next player.

Winner

The first player to complete the word on his card.

Hanukah "Gelt"

Educational purposes: Counting
Object of the game: To collect the greatest number of disks
Number of players: 2 to 4
Equipment: Menorah board
               41 disks (the Hanukah "gelt")
               2 dreidls

Directions for Play

Place the disks on the 41 circles of the menorah. Each player, in turn, spins both dreidls and proceeds according to the letters on which they fall. If both dreidls show the same letter, the player takes the disk which is on the "shammes". If the dreidls fall with two different letters, the player takes the disk from the candle showing the same combination. If there is no longer a disk to match his dreidls, play passes to the next player.

Conclusion

The game is concluded when all the disks have been removed from the menorah. Each player counts his or her disks.

Winner

The player with the greatest number of disks.

NOTE: The letter combinations of נ and ג, ש and ה appear twice.

The Missing Half

Educational purpose: Completing pictures and words.
Object of the game: To match all picture halves.
Number of players: 2
Equipment: 8 picture halves
                 a coin
                 2 playing pieces

Directions for Play

Each player receives 4 picture halves and a playing piece. Each places the playing piece on the square of his choice. Each player, in turn, flips the coin. "Heads" permits moving 2 spaces; "tails" permits moving 1 space. Each player moves in the direction he chooses. Upon reaching a picture-half which matches one of the halves in his hand, he places the card from his hand on the board, to complete the picture. Play then passes to the second player. If he reaches a picture half to which he does not have the matching half, play passes to the second player.

Winner

The first player to create 4 matched pictures with the cards in his hand.

31 — ל״א

In Hebrew, each letter of the alphabet also has a numerical value. In this system, known as "gimetria," the letter "lamed" has a value of 30, and "aleph" equals 1. This game is based on an ancient one, and the "lamed-aleph" refers to the 31 kings in the Land of Canaan conquered by Joshua, the son of Nun. In the ancient Hanukah game, each king was assigned a numerical value, with the higher one conquering the lower one. Our modern version, however, is played with different biblical characters.

Object of the game: To collect all the cards or to collect the number of cards established by the players in advance.
Number of players: 2 to 6
Equipment: 31 cards

Directions for Play

Shuffle the cards and distribute them equally among the players. Remaining cards are set aside.
Each player sets his stack of cards face down, to one side. For each round of play, each player turns over the top card from his stack. The player with the highest card takes all and sets them aside in a separate pile. When the first stack is finished, play continues for each player with the second stack. Anyone who runs out of cards is out of the game.

Winner

The player who wins all the cards or the number which had been decided upon in advance.

Dreidl

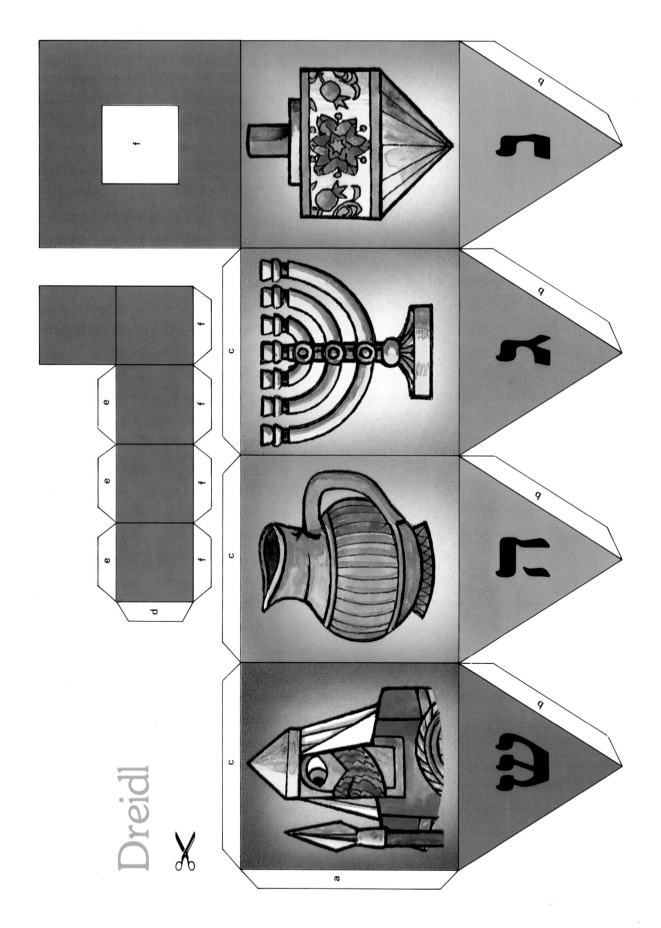

17

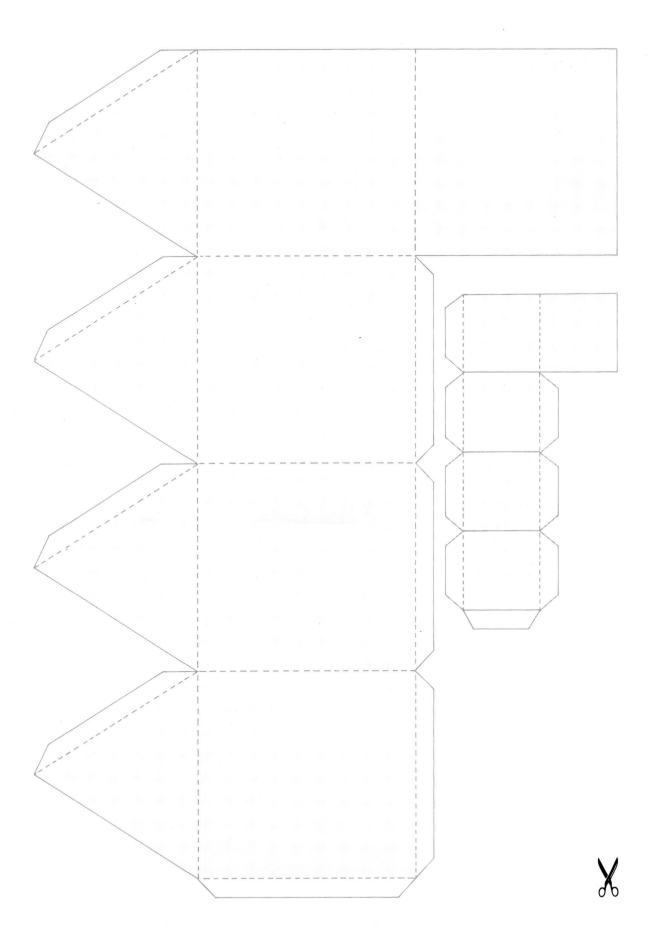

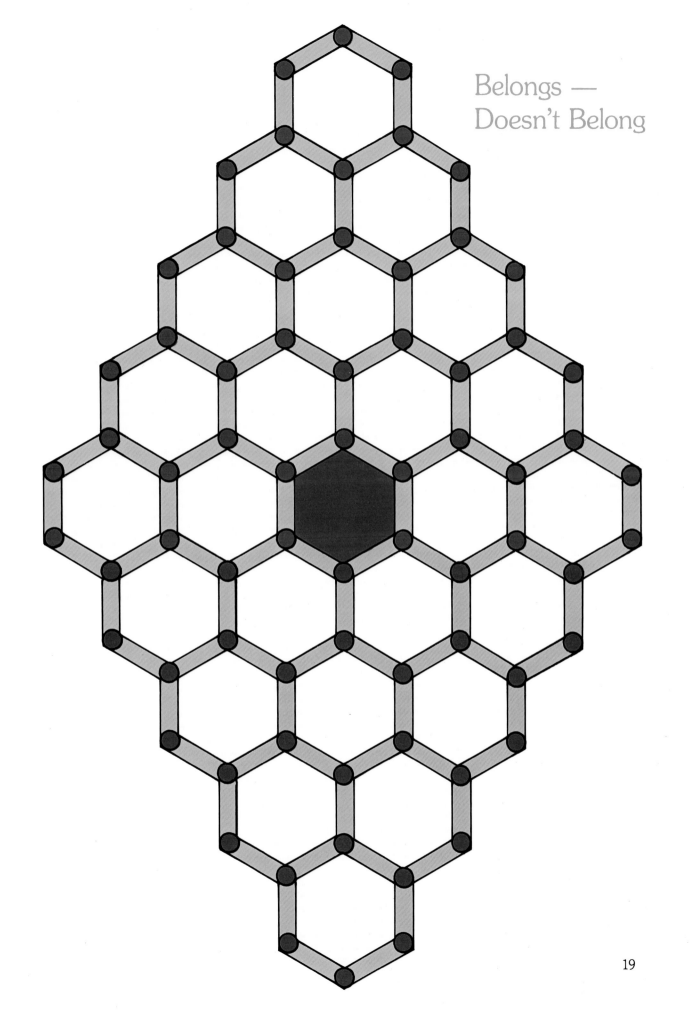

Belongs — Doesn't Belong

2 Dreidls and a Menorah

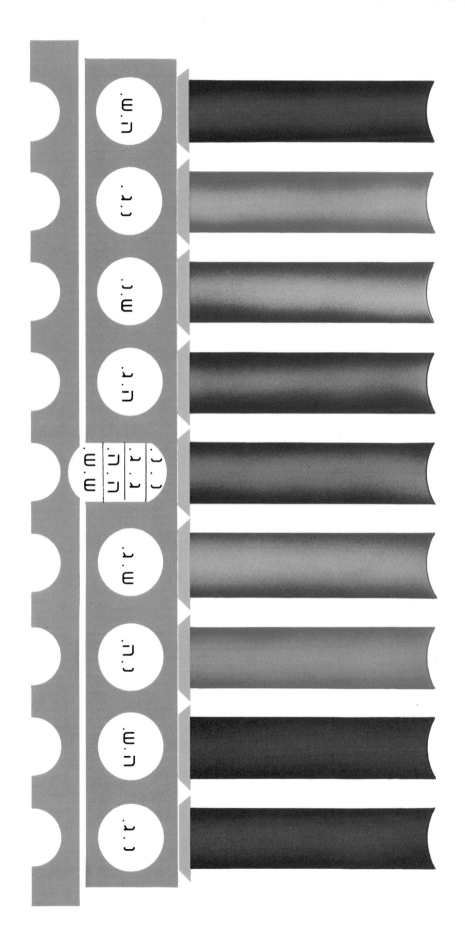

23

2 Dreidls and a Menorah

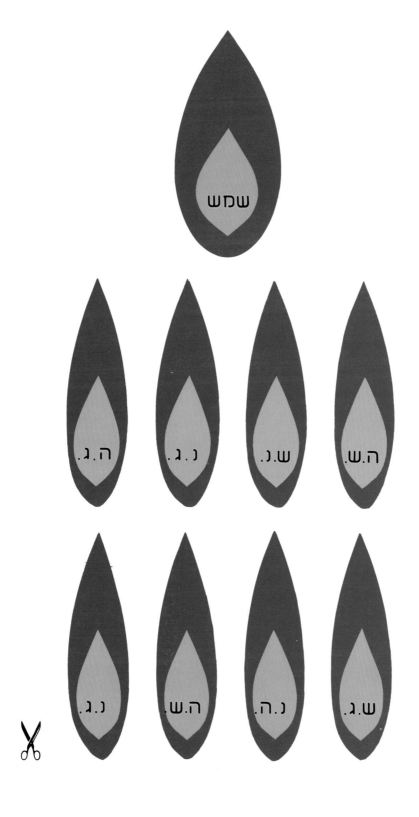

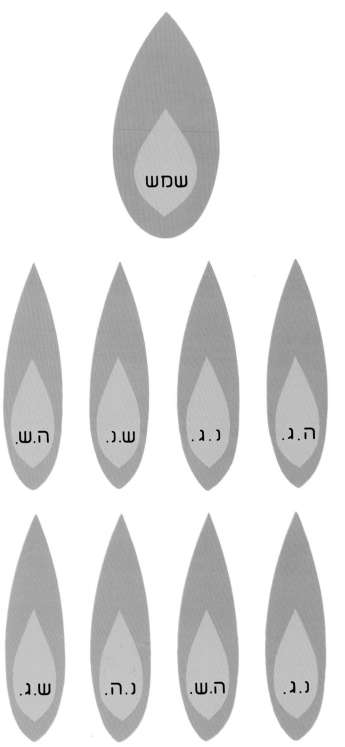

Hanukah Candles

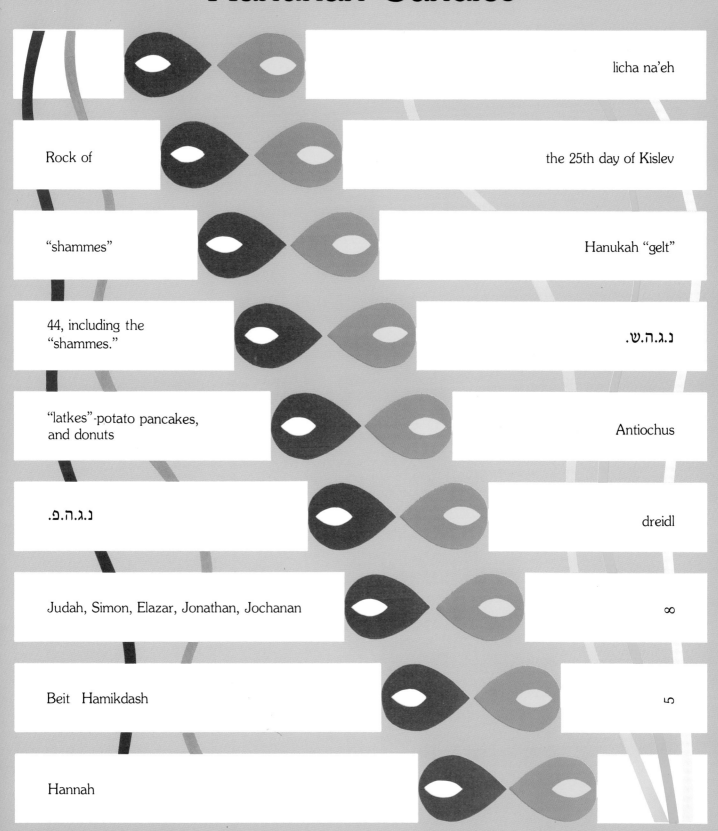

licha na'eh

Rock of

the 25th day of Kislev

"shammes"

Hanukah "gelt"

44, including the "shammes."

נ.ג.ה.ש.

"latkes"-potato pancakes, and donuts

Antiochus

נ.ג.ה.פ.

dreidl

Judah, Simon, Elazar, Jonathan, Jochanan

8

Beit Hamikdash

5

Hannah

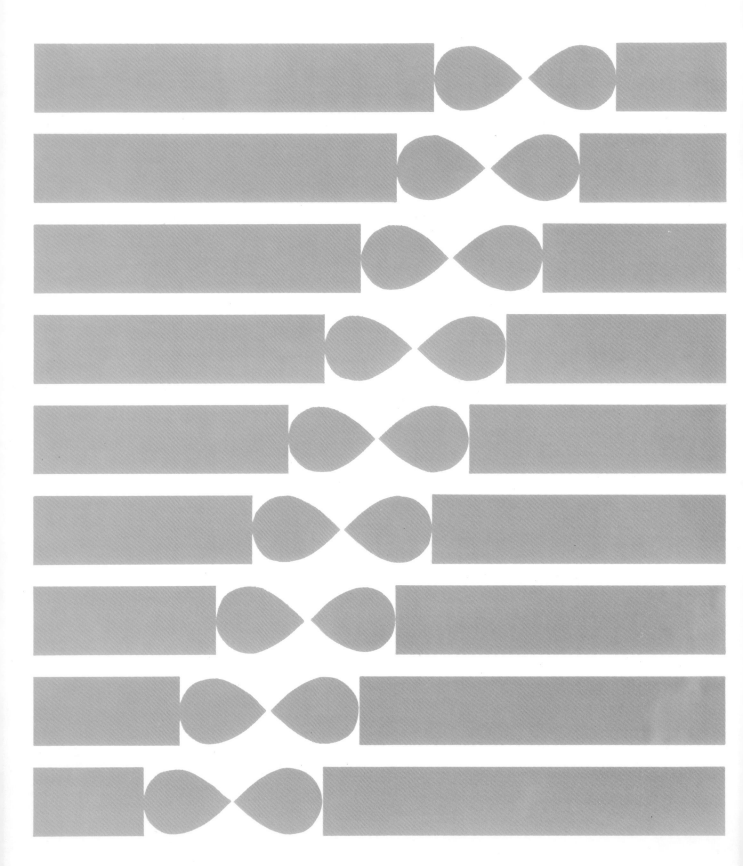

29

Questions for "Hanukah Candles"

What is the meaning of Maoz?

For how many days did the cruse of oil last?

What is the total number of candles lit during the entire holiday?

What are the letters on the dreiple?

What are the letters on the dreidl in Israel?

What is the special Hanuka game?

Which candle is used to light all the others?

How many sons did Mattathias have?

Fill in the blank: "Ma'oz tsur yeshu'ati ———— lishabe'ach."

How do you say "temple" in Hebrew?

What is the name for the money which children receive during Hanukah?

What are the special foods of Hanukah?

Who is the Greek king of the Hanukah story?

What are the names of Mattathias's sons?

What is the date on which Hanukah falls?

Who is the brave mother of the Hanukah story?

Spin & Spell

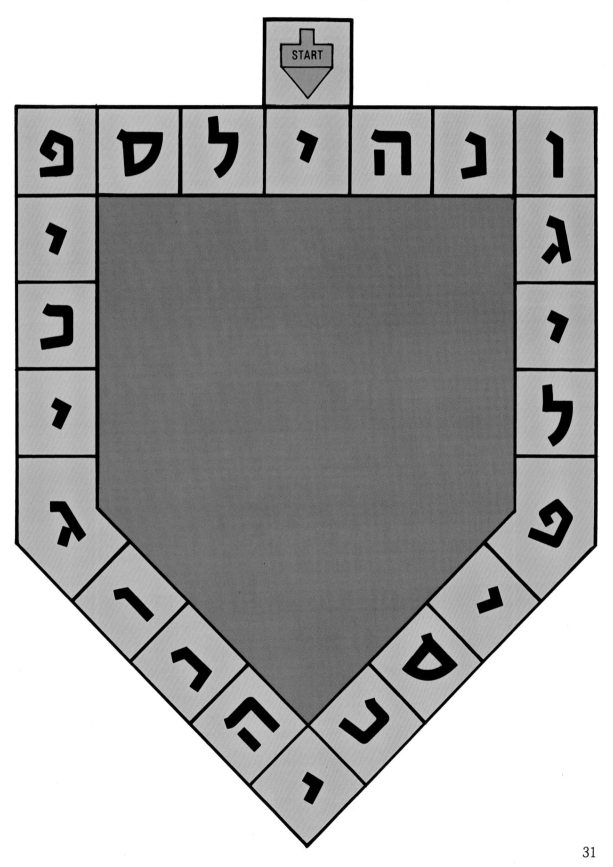

Spin & Spell

סביבון

סְבִיבוֹן

סופגניה

סוּפְגָּנִיָּה

חנוכיה

חֲנוּכִיָּה

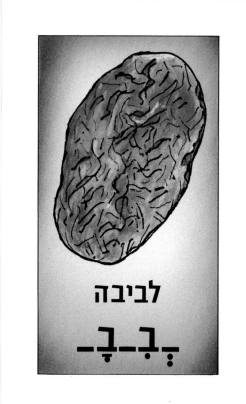

לביבה

לְבִיבָה

Hanukah "Gelt"

The Missing Half

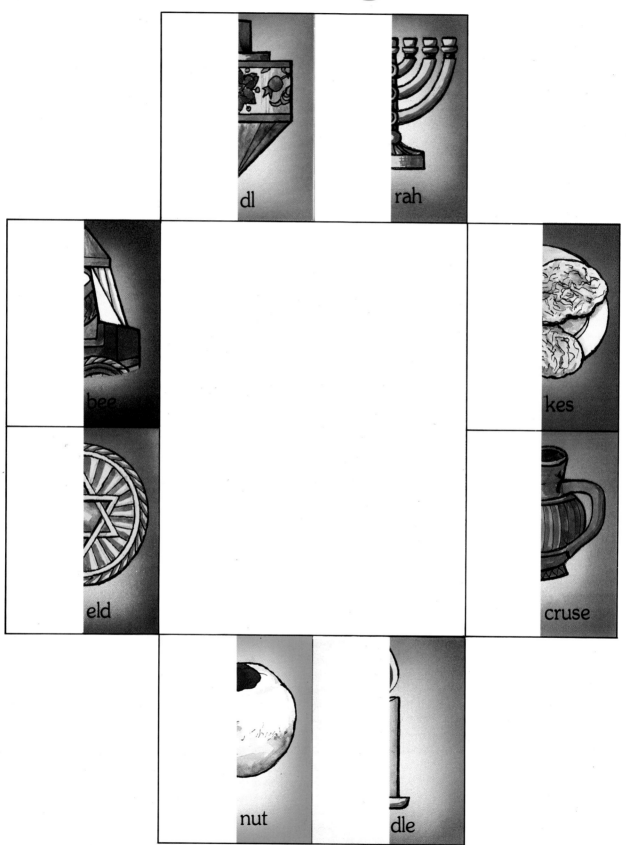

dl

rah

bee

kes

eld

cruse

nut

dle

The Missing Half

Oil

Macca

Drei

Can

Lat

Meno

Dough

Shi

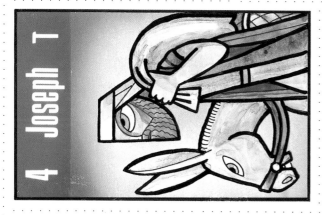

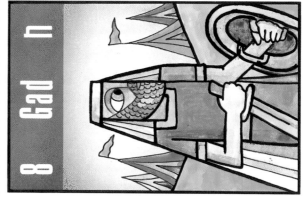

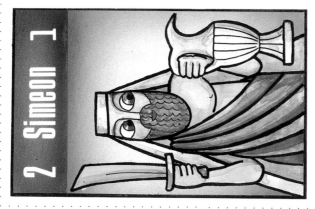

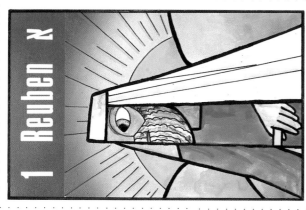

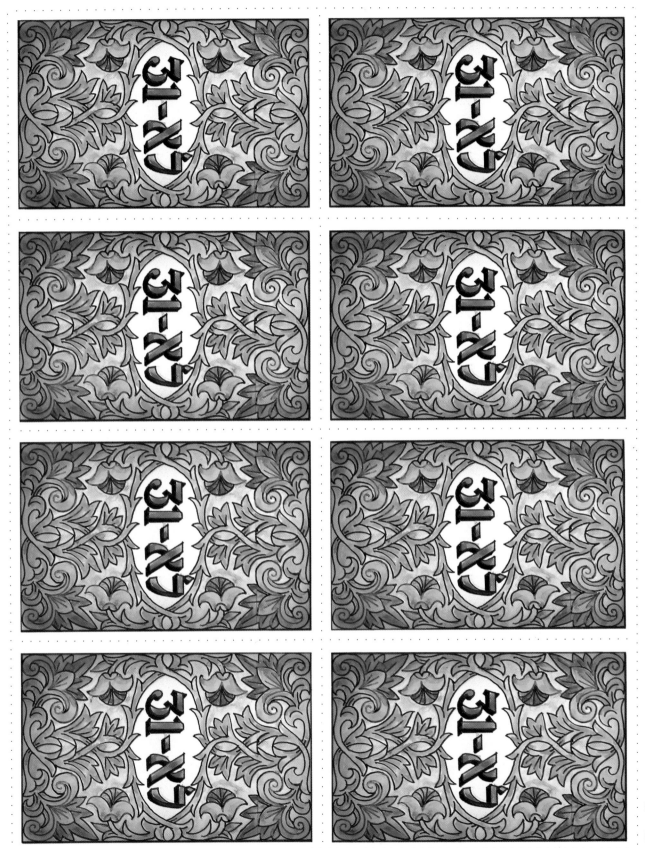

10 Manas'seh מ

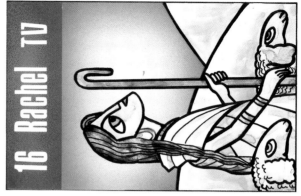

16 Rachel טז

11 Levi יא

15 Leah טו

9 Benjmin ט

14 Ehud יד

12 Asher יב

13 Gideon יג

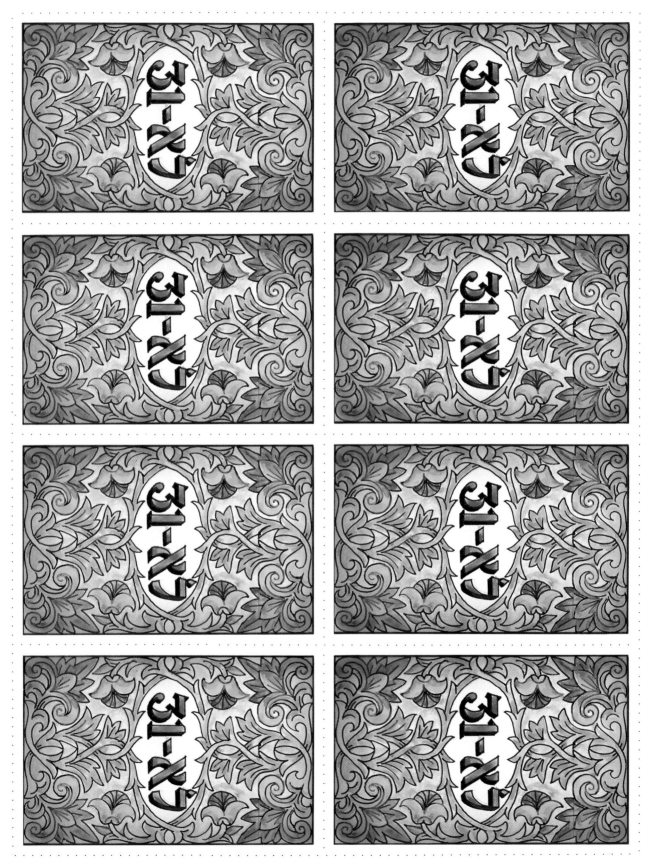

44

20 Jacob ‫כ‬

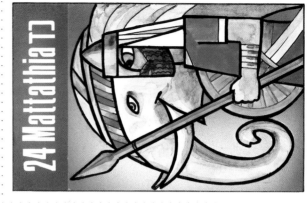

24 Mattathia ‫כד‬

19 Deborah ‫יט‬

23 Abraham ‫כג‬

18 Sarah ‫יח‬

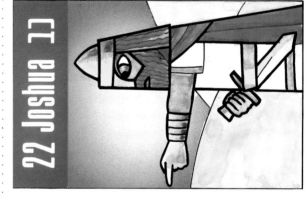

22 Joshua ‫כב‬

17 Rebekah ‫יז‬

21 Isaac ‫כא‬

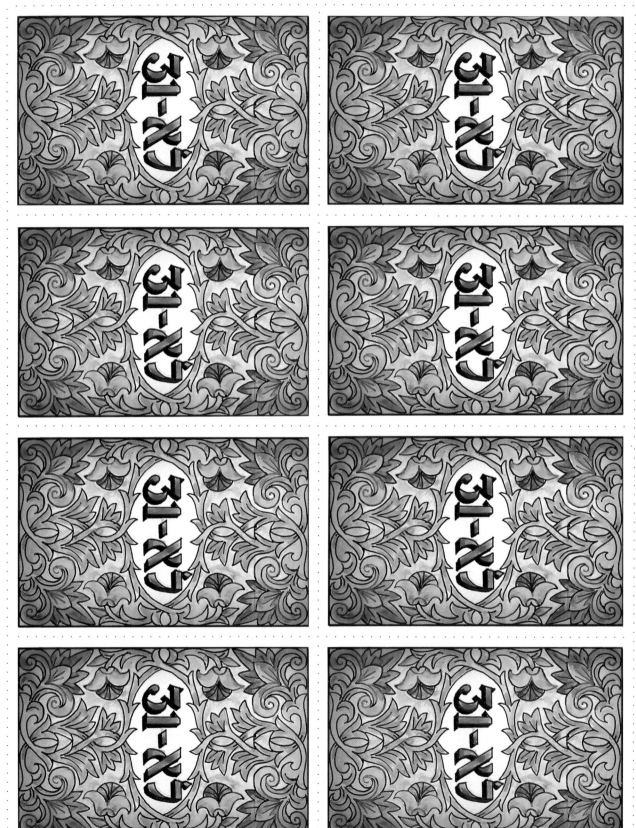

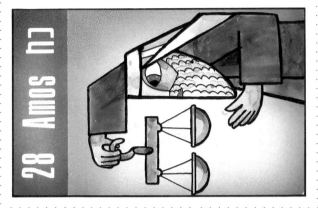

28 Amos נב

לא-31

27 Isaiah כד

30 David ל

26 Jermiah כו

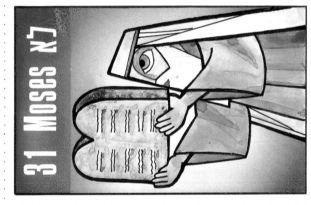

31 Moses לא

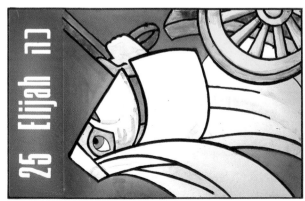

25 Elijah נה

29 Solomon כט

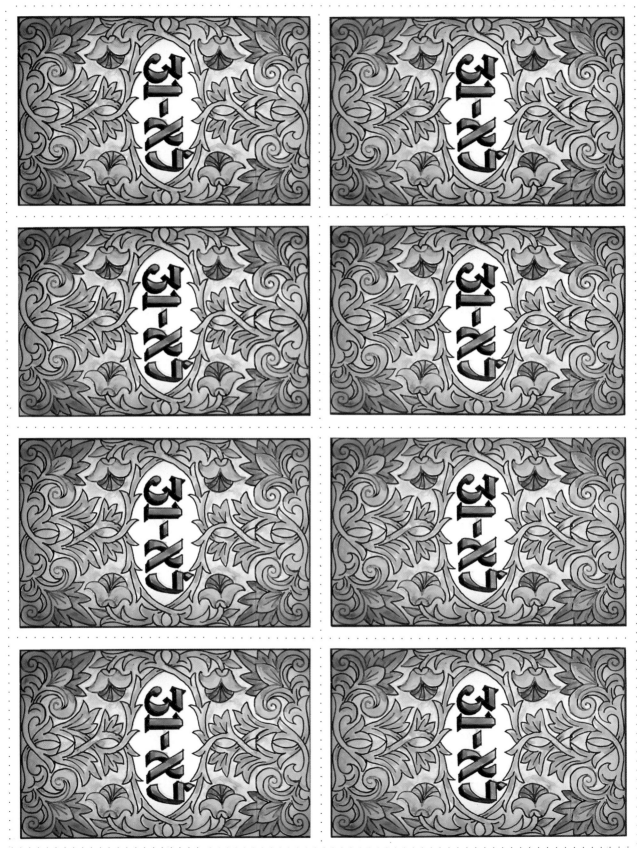